2025

January

Su	Mo	Tu	We	Th	Fr	Sa
			1	2	3	4
5	6	7	8	9	10	11
12	13	14	15	16	17	18
19	20	21	22	23	24	25
26	27	28	29	30	31	

February

Su	Mo	Tu	We	Th	Fr	Sa
						1
2	3	4	5	6	7	8
9	10	11	12	13	14	15
16	17	18	19	20	21	22
23	24	25	26	27	28	

March

Su	Mo	Tu	We	Th	Fr	Sa
						1
2	3	4	5	6	7	8
9	10	11	12	13	14	15
16	17	18	19	20	21	22
23	24	25	26	27	28	29
30	31					

April

Su	Mo	Tu	We	Th	Fr	Sa
		1	2	3	4	5
6	7	8	9	10	11	12
13	14	15	16	17	18	19
20	21	22	23	24	25	26
27	28	29	30			

May

Su	Mo	Tu	We	Th	Fr	Sa
				1	2	3
4	5	6	7	8	9	10
11	12	13	14	15	16	17
18	19	20	21	22	23	24
25	26	27	28	29	30	31

June

Su	Mo	Tu	We	Th	Fr	Sa
1	2	3	4	5	6	7
8	9	10	11	12	13	14
15	16	17	18	19	20	21
22	23	24	25	26	27	28
29	30					

July

Su	Mo	Tu	We	Th	Fr	Sa
		1	2	3	4	5
6	7	8	9	10	11	12
13	14	15	16	17	18	19
20	21	22	23	24	25	26
27	28	29	30	31		

August

Su	Mo	Tu	We	Th	Fr	Sa
					1	2
3	4	5	6	7	8	9
10	11	12	13	14	15	16
17	18	19	20	21	22	23
24	25	26	27	28	29	30
31						

September

Su	Mo	Tu	We	Th	Fr	Sa
	1	2	3	4	5	6
7	8	9	10	11	12	13
14	15	16	17	18	19	20
21	22	23	24	25	26	27
28	29	30				

October

Su	Mo	Tu	We	Th	Fr	Sa
		1	2	3	4	
5	6	7	8	9	10	11
12	13	14	15	16	17	18
19	20	21	22	23	24	25
26	27	28	29	30	31	

November

Su	Mo	Tu	We	Th	Fr	Sa
						1
2	3	4	5	6	7	8
9	10	11	12	13	14	15
16	17	18	19	20	21	22
23	24	25	26	27	28	29
30						

December

Su	Mo	Tu	We	Th	Fr	Sa
	1	2	3	4	5	6
7	8	9	10	11	12	13
14	15	16	17	18	19	20
21	22	23	24	25	26	27
28	29	30	31			

NOTES

NOTES

IMPORTANT DATES
2025

January

February

March

April

May

June

July

August

September

October

November

December

JANUARY
2025

MONDAY	TUESDAY	WEDNESDAY	THURSDAY
		1	2
6	7	8	9
13	14	15	16
20	21	22	23
27	28	29	30

FRIDAY	SATURDAY	SUNDAY	NOTES
3	4	5	
10	11	12	
17	18	19	
24	25	26	
31			

FEBRUARY
2025

MONDAY	TUESDAY	WEDNESDAY	THURSDAY
3	4	5	6
10	11	12	13
17	18	19	20
24	25	26	27

FRIDAY	SATURDAY	SUNDAY	*NOTES*
	1	2	___________
7	8	9	___________
14 Valentine's Day	15	16	___________
21	22	23	___________
28			___________

MARCH
2025

MONDAY	TUESDAY	WEDNESDAY	THURSDAY
3	4	5	6
10	11	12	13
17	18	19	20
S. 31	24	25	26	27

FRIDAY	SATURDAY	SUNDAY	NOTES
	1	2	
7	8	9	
14	15	16	
21	22	23	
28	29	30	

APRIL
2025

MONDAY	TUESDAY	WEDNESDAY	THURSDAY
	1	2	3
7	8	9	10
14	15	16	17
21	22	23	24
28	29	30	1

FRIDAY	SATURDAY	SUNDAY	NOTES
4	5	6	
11	12	13	
18	19	20	
25	26	27	

MAY
2025

MONDAY	TUESDAY	WEDNESDAY	THURSDAY
			1
5	6	7	8
12	13	14	15
19	20	21	22
26	27	28	29

FRIDAY	SATURDAY	SUNDAY	NOTES
2	3	4	
9	10	11 Mother's Day	
16	17	18	
23	24	25	
30	31	1	

JUNE
2025

MONDAY	TUESDAY	WEDNESDAY	THURSDAY
2	3	4	5
9	10	11	12
16	17	18	19
23	24	25	26

FRIDAY	SATURDAY	SUNDAY	NOTES
6	7	8	
13	14 Flag Day	15 Father's Day	
20	21	22	
27	28	29	

JULY
2025

MONDAY	TUESDAY	WEDNESDAY	THURSDAY
	1	2	3
7	8	9	10
14	15	16	17
21	22	23	24
28	29	30	31

FRIDAY	SATURDAY	SUNDAY	NOTES
4 Independence Day	5	6	
11	12	13	
18	19	20	
25	26	27	

AUGUST
2025

MONDAY	TUESDAY	WEDNESDAY	THURSDAY
4	5	6	7
11	12	13	14
18	19	20	21
25	26	27	28

FRIDAY	SATURDAY	SUNDAY	NOTES
1	2	3	
8	9	10	
15	16	17	
22	23	24	
29	30	31	

SEPTEMBER
2025

MONDAY	TUESDAY	WEDNESDAY	THURSDAY
1	2	3	4
8	9	10	11
15	16	17	18
22	23	24	25
29	30		

FRIDAY	SATURDAY	SUNDAY	NOTES
5	6	7	
12	13	14	
19	20	21	
26	27	28	

OCTOBER
2025

MONDAY	TUESDAY	WEDNESDAY	THURSDAY
		1	2
6	7	8	9
13	14	15	16
20	21	22	23
27	28	29	30

FRIDAY	SATURDAY	SUNDAY	NOTES
3	4	5	
10	11	12	
17	18	19	
24	25	26	
31 Halloween			

NOVEMBER
2025

MONDAY	TUESDAY	WEDNESDAY	THURSDAY
3	4	5	6
10	11	12	13
17	18	19	20
24	25	26	27

FRIDAY	SATURDAY	SUNDAY	NOTES
	1	2	
7	8	9	
"Veterans Day" day off			
14	15	16	
21	22	23	
28	29	30	
Black Friday			

DECEMBER
2025

MONDAY	TUESDAY	WEDNESDAY	THURSDAY
1	2	3	4
8	9	10	11
15	16	17	18
22	23	24	25
29	30	31	

FRIDAY	SATURDAY	SUNDAY	NOTES
5	6	7	
12	13	14	
19	20	21	
26	27	28	

Printed in the USA
CPSIA information can be obtained
at www.ICGtesting.com
LVHW080322021124
795330LV00011B/395